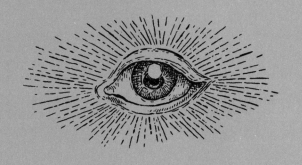

INSTANT MAGIC

SEMRA HAKSEVER

GUIDANCE TO ALL OF LIFE'S QUESTIONS FROM YOUR HIGHER SELF

ORACLE

OH EDITIONS

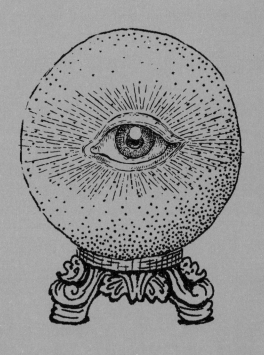

WELCOME
TO THE ORACLE

Within these pages you will find yourself being guided to messages, visualisations, rituals, spells and cosmic tools, all of which have all been created with the desire to bring instant magic into your life.

I believe magic comes in many forms and always with the sole purpose of shifting energy and inspiring you to vibrate at a higher frequency. My intention for you, when using this Oracle, is to see each page as a magical invitation from the cosmos. As you flick through the pages, trust in the subconscious mind, and have faith that the Universe and the Oracle are working together to guide you to what you need to see at that exact time.

Allow the Oracle to gift you with intuitive guidance and bring inspiration. Willingly accept the prompts to love and be kind to yourself, and bear in mind that any triggers and resistance that you feel when landing on a particular page might be the very reason you landed there. The divine timing of seeing a particular message at the right time can be a very powerful and life-changing thing.

There have been many times in my life where I have turned to Oracles and pendulums for guidance and intuitive confirmations, so it is an honour to be able to create an Oracle with my own magical twist!

May this Oracle connect you with all the wisdom that is within and awaken your magic.

Love,
Semra X

HOW TO USE THE ORACLE

As with all mystical tools, it is important to energetically connect with the Oracle before you ask your question. To do this:

1. Hold the Oracle in your less dominant hand and then knock it three times with your dominant hand. This will clear it of anyone else's energy and connect your energy to it.

2. Next, hold it in both hands and think of your question, making sure you focus on just one thing at a time. You may ask this out loud, whisper it to the Oracle or close your eyes and visualise what you wish to ask in your mind.

    For superpower, you may want to chant:

    'Magic Oracle, bring to me,
    magic and wisdom for me to see.
    Bring me the answers that I seek,
    guidance and magic for me to keep.
    I call upon your sacred power,
    to show me the answers I desire.'

3. Then turn the book three times towards you in a clockwise direction.

4. At this point, how you are guided to your message is up to you – you may wish you just randomly open it up to a page, or you might want to flick through the pages back and forth and left to right until it feels like the right time to open it, or you may wish to start in the middle and fan the pages out. The main thing is to do whatever feels right. The important thing is to trust that you are being energetically guided, and you will land exactly where you need to.

6

The Oracle may direct you to a message – often these messages tend to speak to us immediately. However, if you don't connect with the message straight away, try to intuitively tune in to it. Take a picture of it and look at it again a little later – chances are it will resonate then.

Know that these messages have the power to shift energy and help you see more clearly.

If the Oracle takes you to a visualisation, you are being called to connect to the magic and wisdom within, and this should serve as a reminder that you have the power inside of you. All you have to do is close your eyes and visualise being somewhere else – whether that may be seeing a future version of yourself with all of your manifestations coming into fruition, or calling in on the power of your imagination. This is a wonderful reminder that magic lies within all of us.

Or the Oracle might guide you to a ritual. I know that some of these may not seem particularly instant, but chances are that the Oracle is suggesting the spell so that you take some time out and slow down. We live such hectic lives and the power of a ritual is that they present us with a moment in time to slow down and be fully conscious of what we are doing. In my experience, there is nothing like a ritual to call for you to be fully present in the moment. Remember: a ritual is a moment of complete and utter consciousness of dedicated time to a specific outcome.

Finally, you may land on a symbol. In this case, all you need to do is close your eyes and think of all the things the symbol means to you. This is a moment when the Oracle wants you to tune in to your intuition and flex your psychic powers.

Disclaimer:
If for some reason you land on a spell and you don't connect to it, please don't force it. Just close your eyes and ask the Oracle again.

INGREDIENTS
AND TOOLS

Due to the nature of this Oracle being based on instant magic, I have kept the magical ingredients to a minimum. However, there are a few things that you will need for the spells – many of which are easily accessible:

A magnet

A key

A shiny coin

Candles (in different colours if possible)

Different coloured thread

Hot charcoal

An incense burner or metal dish

A glass jar

Bay leaves

Cloves

Olive or almond oil

Sunflower oil

Thyme

Mint

Chamomile

Pepper

Celery seeds

Lemons

Salt

Rosemary

Sage

Sugar

Cinnamon sticks

Honey

A pen and paper

Vinegar

Matches or a lighter

A small mirror

A gold or silver ring

A potted plant

Parchment paper

Nails

Sit with a plant and give it a name. Touch it, talk to it, caress it, study it and get lost in the wonder of its green beauty. Feel its magical vibrations and thank it for being alive. (If you don't have a plant, take this as your sign to go and buy one immediately, if not sooner!)

You are surrounded
by a team of guardian
angels, who are sending
you signs to let you
know that you are loved
and protected. When
you landed on this page,
they all high-fived and
cheered! They want to
remind you to look out
for the signs that they
are sending to you.

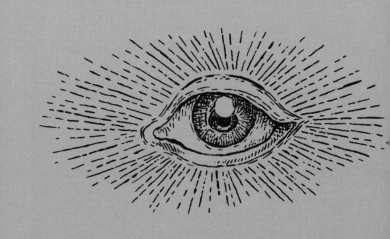

The Oracle wants
you to be clear on your
intentions. Chew on
some celery seeds to
bring the magic of
ultimate focus.

Your guardians want you to know that you are loved, and you are protected. Close your eyes and feel their presence.

INTUITION CHALLENGE: A DOOR

What does a door mean to you?

How do you connect with this image?

If you are really stuck,
turn to page 508 for some psychic prompts.

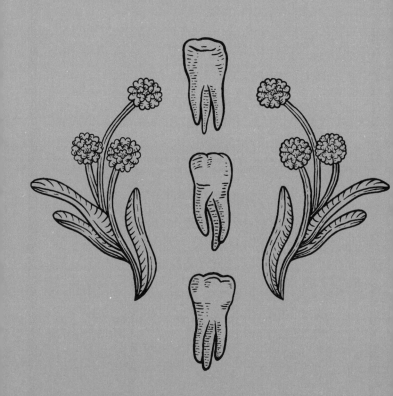

Relax and act like you already have whatever you are manifesting, and it will flow to you.

ENERGY MAINTENANCE
IS REQUIRED

You have landed on this page because stagnant energy may be blocking you and your energy field. Sometimes when we go through a challenging time, or have been hanging around some heavy energy, our vibe can need a shake up to get things moving again.

REMEMBER
Sounds are vibrations,
and noise shifts frequencies.

YOU WILL NEED

something that can be used to make some
noise, such as a bell, sound bowl, drum,
a box of matches, a pot and a wooden
spoon or just simply clap with your hands!

1. Sit or stand with both feet on the
    ground and get ready to shake, bang,
    or clap and create a loud sound to
    shift energy around your body. If you
    feel like your voice has been blocked
    and you've not been speaking up for
    yourself lately, make the noise around
    your throat.

2. As you make these sounds, close
    your eyes and visualise the energy
    shifting. See if it has a colour and
    imagine it evaporating away; picture
    it disappearing and feel the energy
    transforming into a silver sparkly
    light. Notice how refreshing this feels
    and the lightness that it brings. You
    may also want to extend this ritual
    and make some noise around your
    house, including under the bed, in
    cupboards and drawers, just as you
    would with a sage cleanse.

Imagine the cutest, fluffiest kitten. Think about how gentle and loving you would be towards this adorable little creature.

Now use the same energy on yourself, and treat yourself just as you would this sweet little kitten.

INTUITION CHALLENGE: A RING

What does a ring mean to you?

How do you connect with this image?

If you are really stuck, turn to page 508 for some psychic prompts.

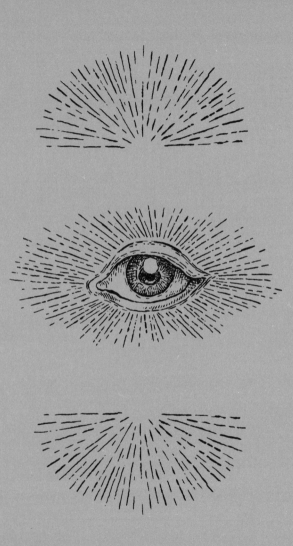

Create some space
in your life to sit
in silence and observe
your feelings.

Focus on the rhythm of
your breath, follow its
journey as you
breathe in and out.
Take note of how
you feel.

What comes up?
Remember to try not to
overthink or judge, just
be still and listen.

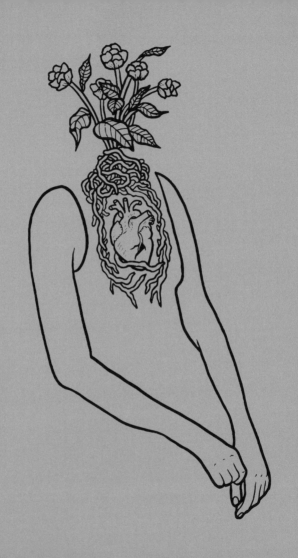

MAJOR
BREAKTHROUGH
INCOMING!

You are carrying
around some old
guilt and shame.
It is time to release it.

✦

Let it go.

SPEAK LESS AND LISTEN MORE.

Something needs to
be healed and this is
holding you back.

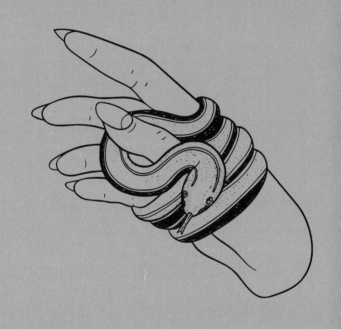

ARE YOU PAYING ATTENTION TO THE SIGNS?

INTUITION
INCOMING

Your intuition has led you to this page
and it is calling you to tap into its power.

a pen and paper (optional)

1. Close your eyes and take a few gentle, slow, deep breaths.

2. When your breathing returns to normal and you are feeling still and calm, use your index finger and third finger and start to gently tap on your third eye.

3. Do this for a few moments and take note of the first thing that comes into your mind. This could be in the form of a direct message, a shape, a colour or a feeling in your body.

4. If you like you can then get a pen and paper, close your eyes and write with your less dominant hand (writing with your less dominant hand activates the right side of the brain, which tunes in to the subconscious and helps turn up your psychic abilities).

FROM THE DESK OF INSTANT MAGIC ORACLE

NO. 001

DATE: Now

EXPIRY:

PERMISSION SLIP

You don't have to be perfect.

IX
PERMISSION
SLIP

START NOW

The same tests will
keep showing up until
the lessons have
been learnt.

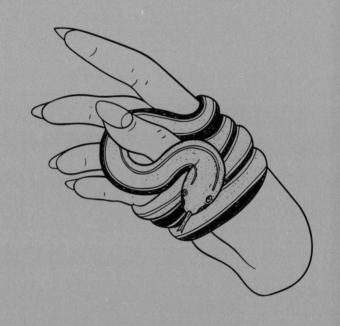

SLOW DOWN!

You're moving
too fast.

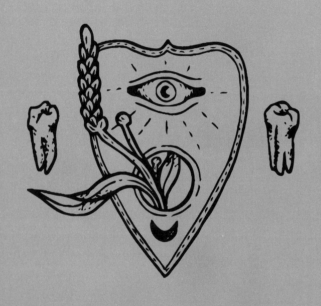

MANIFEST
EXPANSION.

Practice complete
compassion towards
EVERYONE for the
next 24 hours.

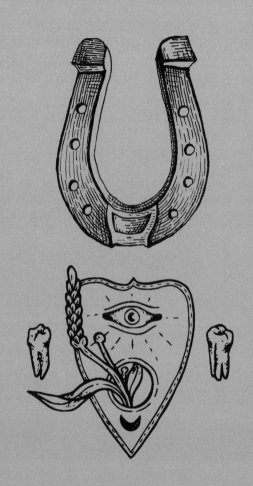

BLESSINGS INCOMING

When you bless your blessings, you magnify them. Use the power of your blessings to call in more.

YOU WILL NEED

two cinnamon sticks, yellow string or wool, a candle, matches or a lighter

1. Take two sticks of cinnamon and some yellow string.

2. Tie the string around the centre of the cinnamon sticks, and knot them together, with the knot facing towards you.

3. Tie nine knots in total and with each knot, count one of your blessings.

4. Know that one of the cinnamon sticks stands for the blessings you already have and the other one represents all that you are calling in.

5. Once the knots have been tied, burn the cinnamon sticks at both ends and speak your wishes to the smoke.

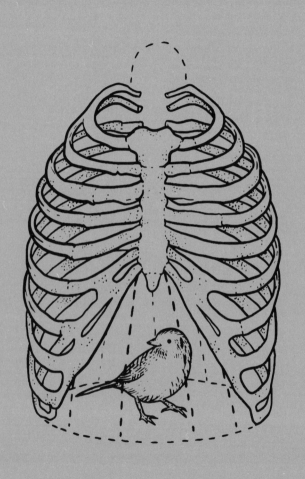

The Oracle dares
you to have so much
confidence in the
Universe having your
back, that you stop
getting upset when
things don't go
your way.

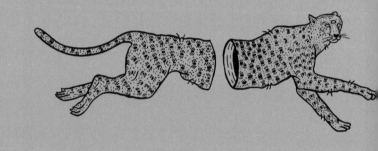

ENERGY LEAK ALERT

You are here because you are being called to take a look at your energy flow. Tired, drained, frustrated? It's time to do something about it.

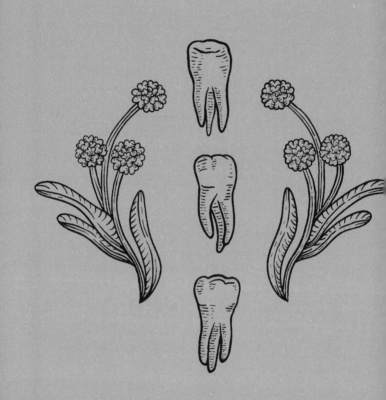

Unfriend, unfollow,
block and move on.

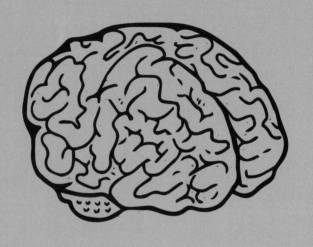

Check in with what you
are consuming, in your
body and your mind.

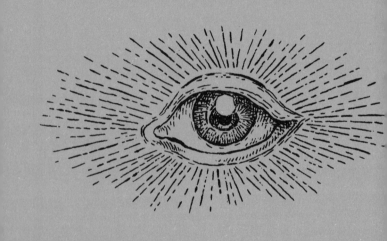

DETACH

The answer to your question is in a book.
Pick up the first book you see (not this one!).

1. Close your eyes and think of your
    question. Allow the book to fall open
    on a random page, and, with your
    eyes closed, guide and point your
    index finger in a circle around the
    open pages and continue to ask your
    question aloud.

2. When it feels right, open your eyes
    and see where your finger is pointing.

3. Here lies your answer.

OBSTACLE REMOVER

Obstacles may be getting in the way
of what you have been calling in.

YOU WILL NEED

a bowl or jar for soaking, salt, a piece of string

1. Fill the bowl or jar with water.
   Add the salt and give it a stir.

2. Take the piece of string and soak
   it in the salt water for an hour or
   overnight.

3. Take the string out and tie it in
   a tight knot. As you tie the knot, think
   of your problem or obstacle.

4. Allow it to dry, either for an hour
   or let it dry overnight.

5. Once it has dried, spend some time
   undoing the knot. As the knot loosens
   the obstacle will begin to release.

6. As soon as the knot is untied the
   obstacle will be removed.

YOU DESERVE
GOOD THINGS.

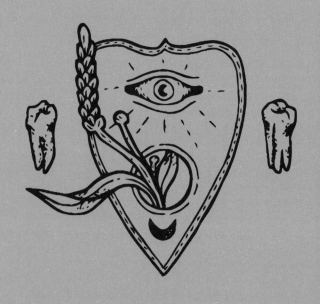

Trust in the ever-unfolding mystery of the Universe.

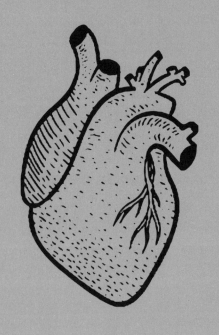

Experiencing all of your emotions is a superpower. Answer the following questions:

The last time I felt happy _____

The last time I felt scared _____

The last time I was surprised _____

The last time I felt sad _____

The last time I was angry _____

The last time I felt pure joy _____

The last time I was excited _____

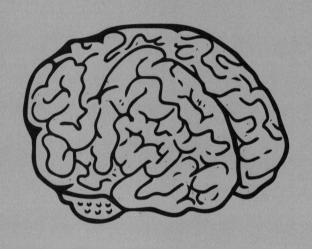

For assistance with
making a clear decision,
click your fingers
10 times around the top
of your head in a
clockwise direction.

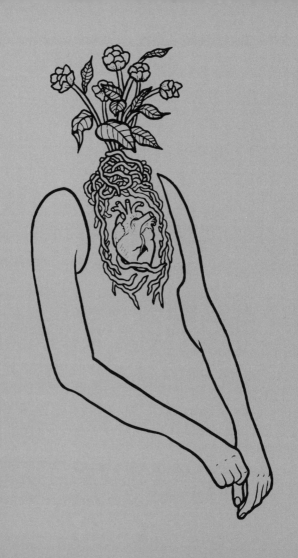

The time has come
to release the fear
of pleasing everyone.

ATTACHMENT ISSUES

There is something in your life that you are attached to and
it is time to detach yourself from it. This could be a person,
a situation, a limiting self-belief, or a pattern of behaviour.
It is time to cut the cord. When we remove what is no longer
serving us in magic, we create room for what we wish to call in.

So think about what you wish to remove and what you
would like to replace it with.

YOU WILL NEED

a piece of string, a white candle, matches or a lighter

1. Tie a knot on the left side of the string and as you do so, think of what it is you wish to banish. Keep in mind that it is always a good idea to banish with love rather than anger or frustration.

2. Notice how the tighter you pull the knot the lighter you feel.

3. Then tie a knot on the right side, and as you tie this knot, really feel what you wish to call in. Feel the empowering energy it will bring.

4. As you pull the knot tighter, imagine it coming closer to you.

5. When you feel ready and have a clear mind, light the candle, hold the centre of the string over the flame, and as the string burns, say the words:

> 'Severing cords away from me,
> I call in the powers that be.
> Magic flame, release this negative energy away from me, and with love I release what is tied to me. No harm is done to anyone, I call in the most positive outcome. So be it.'

You can burn the rest of the negative side and keep the knot of what you are calling in. Place it on your altar or on a window facing east.

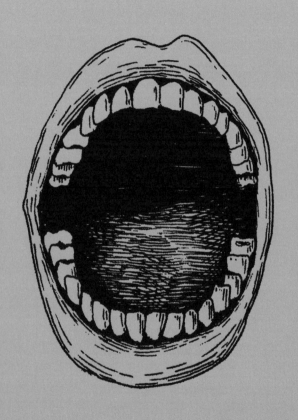

IT IS OK TO HAVE
AN OPINION.

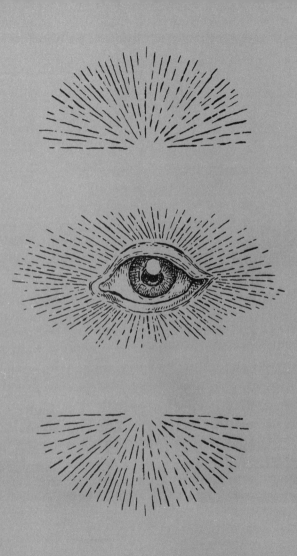

Creating distance
from this situation
will bring clarity.

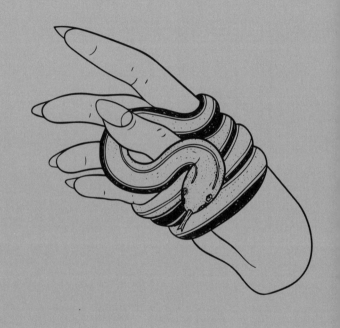

Soon you will understand why your timing was perfect and why things worked out the way they did.

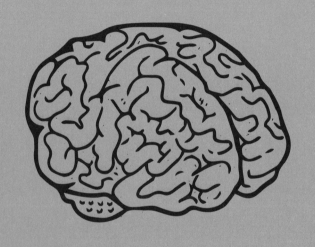

THINK BIGGER!

SEND ME A SIGN

YOU WILL NEED
a bay leaf, a pen, a candle, matches or a lighter

1. Write the question you need answered
    on a bay leaf.

2. Hold it over a flame, and as it burns
    say the incantation:

    'Bay leaf, bay leaf, answer me.
    Send me a smoke signal so I can see.'

If the bay leaf burns bright and easily
then your answer is a yes.

If the bay leaf doesn't catch fire easily and
refuses to burn, then your answer is a no.

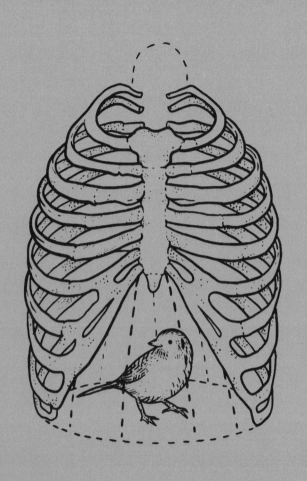

BE TRUE TO YOURSELF.

Let go of your need to have control. It is only when you surrender that you can release.

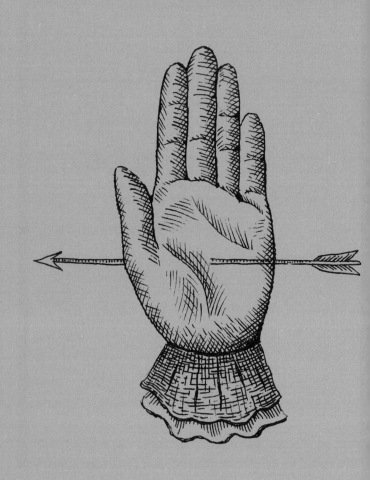

Stop expecting
something bad
to happen.

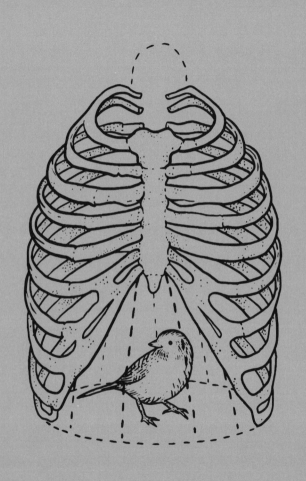

REPEAT
11 TIMES:

'I am worthy of
good things.'

METAL MAGIC

✦

Call in on the power of this magical
element to draw luck your way.

YOU WILL NEED
a potted plant, a gold or silver ring

1. Put a flourishing potted plant facing
   north in your home (ideally on a
   windowsill or outside). Place a gold
   or silver ring in the pot.

2. Think of a wish. This works best with
   a brand-new wish, so something you've
   not had on your intention list before.

3. In the morning, take the piece of
   jewellery and put it back on, and as
   you do this, say:

'Magical golden/silver ring of mine,
bring me luck and wishes combined.
As I wear you every day,
bring my new intention my way.
This or better, I understand.
I trust in the Universe,
with this ring on my hand.'

Shhhhhhh,
I know the secret
to manifesting:
Believe it's
already yours.

HAVE FAITH
IN YOUR
EVOLUTION.

REMINDER:

There is absolutely no need to feel guilty for creating boundaries to protect your energy.

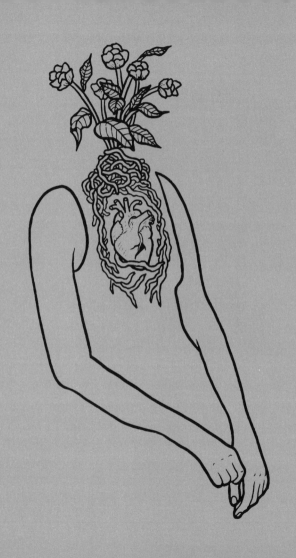

MOON WATER

You are being called to connect
to the moon's current energy.
NB: You can check the moon's cycle
on the internet and on various apps dedicated to
the moon.

YOU WILL NEED

a glass jar filled with some filtered water

1. Leave the jar outside overnight to
   soak up the moon's energy.

2. Check the moon's cycle and do the
   following accordingly:

✧ If the moon is full, drink the water
   and make a wish.

✧ If the moon is waning, pour the water
   over your hands and wash your hands
   of what you wish to say goodbye to.

✧ If the moon is new or waxing, it is
   time to manifest. Drink the water,
   and with each sip, set an intention.

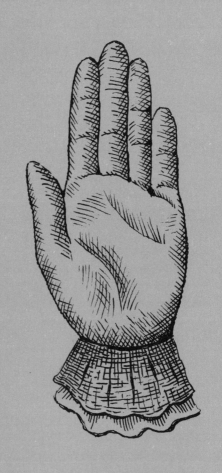

Remember how
far you've come.

Stop trying to convince
others of your worth:
if they don't see it,
they don't deserve it.

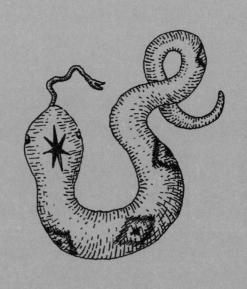

111

By the power of synchronicity you have landed on page 111. These magic numbers are going to bring you MEGA POSITIVE VIBRATIONS.

Opening the Oracle on page 111 is a sign that everything is going to be ok. You are exactly where you need to be.

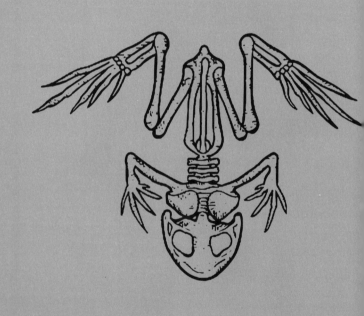

MAJOR TRANSITION INCOMING.

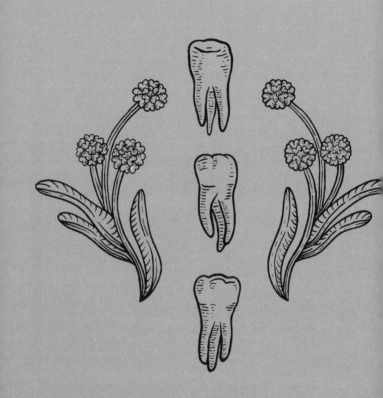

Stop underestimating
how powerful your
gift is – embrace it
and share it with
the world.

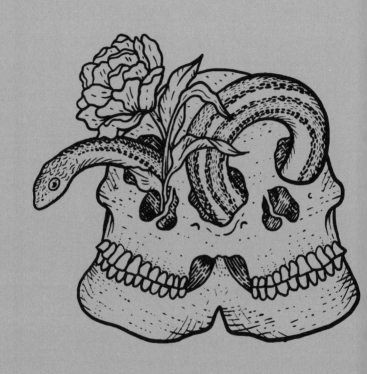

HEALING
IS HAPPENING.

NEW GUIDE

There is a new guide in town
and they want to connect.

YOU WILL NEED
a candle, matches or a lighter

1. Light a candle facing east and say:

'Spirit guide, spirit guide, come to me,
Send me signs or a signal for me to see.
Vision protection and courage,

Whatever it may be –
I'm open to guidance.
So mote it be.'

2. Remember to keep your eyes peeled –
    the signs, symbols and sychronicities
    can present themselves to you in all
    sorts of ways.

3. Look out for random thoughts that
    pop into your head, things may
    instantly align, and plans can be
    delayed or cancelled.

4. Be open to intuitively decoding the
    way these magical messages are being
    sent to you.

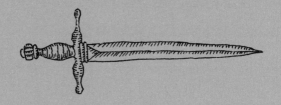

HEAL AND RELEASE

Sometimes when things feel stagnant and slow
it can mean that the Universe is gifting you with
a little bit of time to heal, release or overcome
a challenging moment in your life.

You have been guided here because you may be
feeling ready to get things moving and push
forward with your plans.

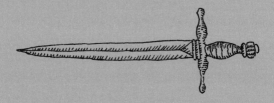

a black pen, a piece of paper, some salt,
a bottle of vinegar

1.   Write in the centre of the paper
     what you wish to release.

2.   Cover the words on the paper
     with the salt.

3.   Focus on the paper and feel the
     salt absorbing what you have
     written down.

4.   When you feel ready, tip the salt
     into the bottle of vinegar.

5.   Rip the piece of paper up into tiny
     pieces and throw it in the bin.

6.   Put the lid back on the vinegar
     and shake the bottle.

7.   As you shake it, feel the release
     getting lighter and lighter;
     feel the hindrance disintegrating
     in the vinegar.

8.   When it feels right, pour the vinegar
     down the sink.

9.   Turn on the tap and wash it away.

10. Know that you are free of this burden
     and things should start moving again.

DON'T
OVERTHINK IT.

IT'S NOT ALL LOVE AND LIGHT.

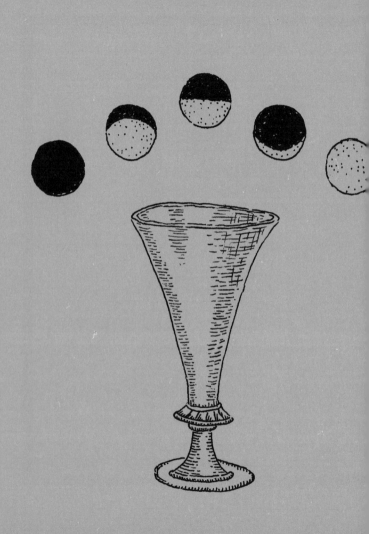

FULL MOON RITUAL

Make your wishes come true with
the following full moon ritual.

YOU WILL NEED

a magnet, seven cloves, a yellow envelope or
piece of fabric or paper for wrapping

1. On the next full moon, go outside
    and lay out the magnet surrounded
    by the cloves.

2. Look up at the moon and make
    your wish.

3. Bring these items in before sunrise
    and wrap them in your yellow item.
    As you wrap them, focus on your wish
    magnetising towards you.

4. Carry this magical vessel with you
    for the next moon cycle and your
    wish should come true before the
    next full moon.

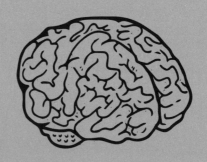

You are allowed to
change your opinion.

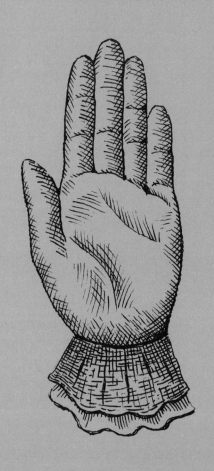

ACT NOW.

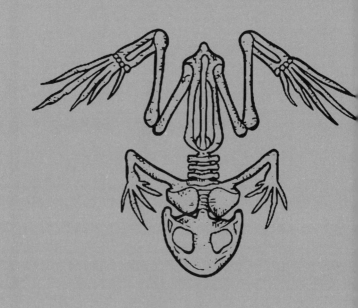

The Oracle is unable
to help on this occasion.

Your power is immense
right now, use it wisely.

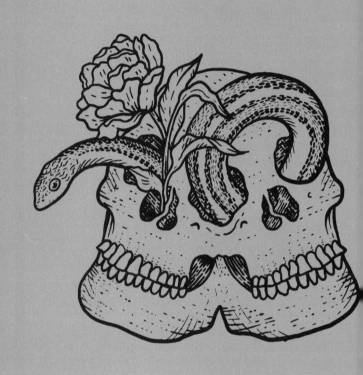

You can always
change your mind.

Watch out for
those who dare to
dim your magic.

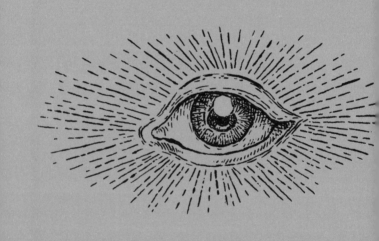

No need to rush,
sometimes its better
to walk than to run.

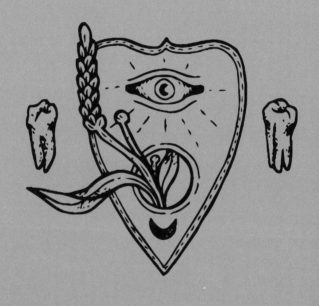

TIME
WILL TELL.

THERE IS NO WRONG WAY OF DOING ANYTHING.

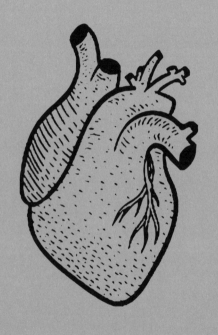

There will be an
important message
for you in your
horoscope today.

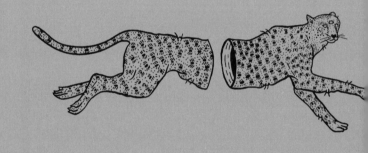

The Oracle is telling you to mix up your daily routine to see major changes and energy shifts.

Your instincts are
right this time.

YOU DESERVE
A TREAT.

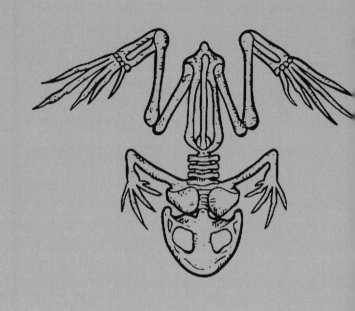

It won't always
feel like this.

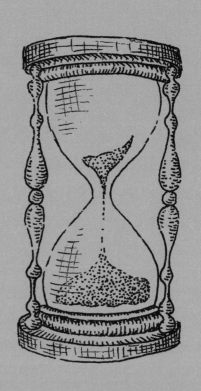

Everything is
constantly evolving.

VERY SOON
IT WILL ALL
BE WORTH IT.

BIG MEGA
MASSIVE PAY-OFF
INCOMING.

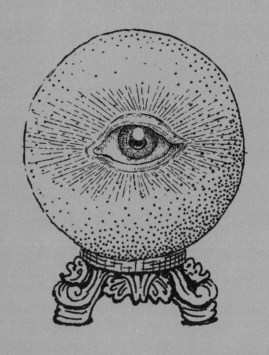

The Oracle says:
ask again and this time
really focus on what you
want guidance with.

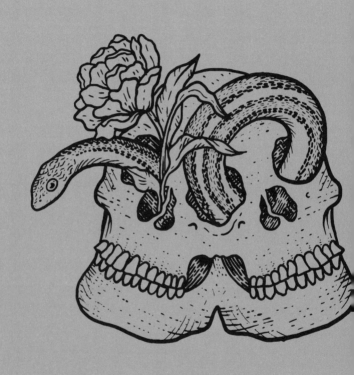

If it doesn't feel aligned
then the answer is no.

INTUITION
CHALLENGE:
A SUITCASE

What does a suitcase mean to you?

How do you connect with this image?

If you are really stuck,
turn to page 508 for some psychic prompts.

For true alignment:
always start with
the question,
'Am I being true
to myself?'

MORE GRATITUDE,
=
MORE BLESSINGS.

TRAVEL IS
ADVISED.

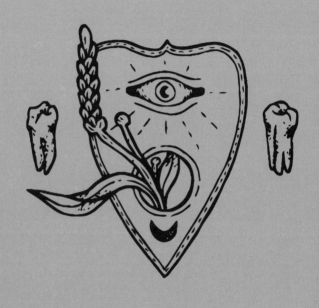

Manifest beyond your dreams. Close your eyes and visualise what life will be like once all of your manifestations have come true.

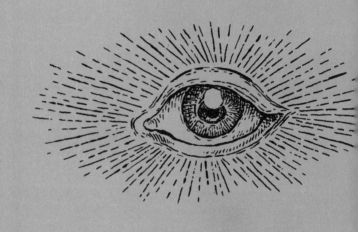

Carry on doing what
you do, you never know
who you are inspiring.

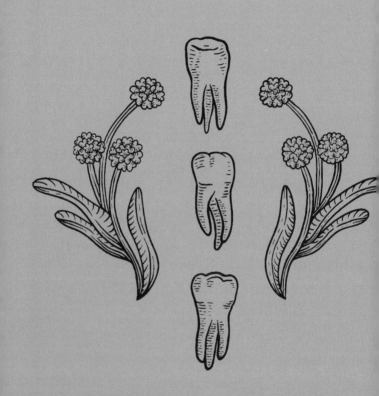

Set your intentions
with precision.

The past version
of you is so proud of
how far you've come.

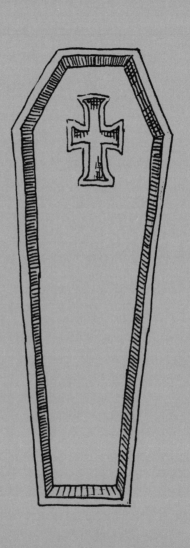

INTUITION
CHALLENGE:
A COFFIN

What does a coffin mean to you?

How do you connect with this image?

If you are really stuck, turn to page 508 for some psychic prompts.

LOOK IN THE MIRROR AND REPEAT THREE TIMES:

I am a living magnet and I love attracting happiness, success, prosperity, peace and an abundance of magic into my life.

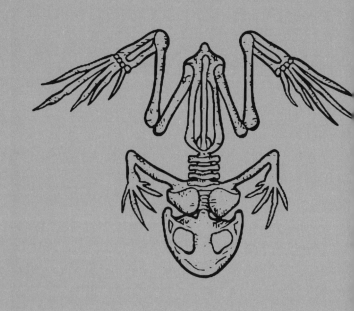

THIS PAGE IS A RED FLAG.

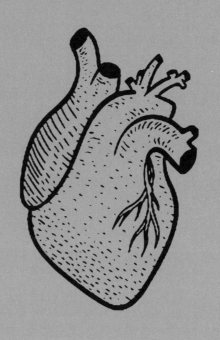

CHALLENGE:

Love yourself as much
as you want someone
else to.

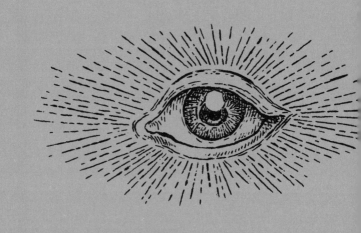

The Oracle wants to remind you that some of the best days of your life haven't happened yet.

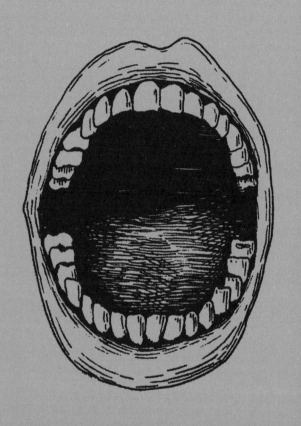

When you can't control what is happening, challenge yourself to control how you respond. This is where you will find the power.

You have the power to
shift energy. Remember
that wherever you go,
or who you are with,
your magical energy
adds value and sparkle
to those who are in
your company.

INTUITION CHALLENGE: SCALES

What does a set of scales mean to you?

How do you connect with this image?

If you are really stuck,
turn to page 509 for some psychic prompts.

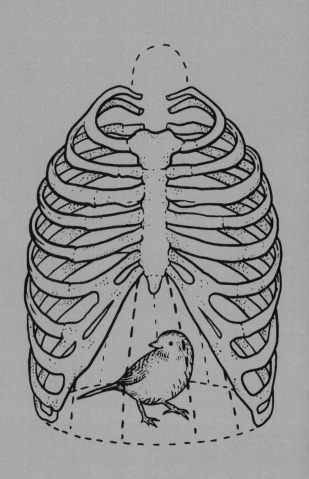

IT'S TIME FOR
A QUICK RELEASE:

1. Make a fist with your right hand and place it on your heart centre.

2. Cover your right hand with your left hand.

3. Close your eyes.

4. Say out loud 10 times:

> 'I release what doesn't serve me,
> I welcome in love.'

Trust the vibes
you are getting.

Remember:
energy doesn't lie.

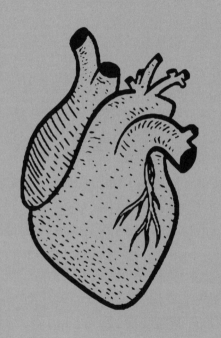

THE ORACLE WISHES TO DELIVER YOU ROMANCE

This spell works both for those who are in relationships and those who are single.

YOU WILL NEED

two items that belong together (such as a salt and pepper shaker, chopsticks, a knife and fork etc), pink ribbon or twine

1. Stand your chosen objects about 30 cm (12 in) apart and tie the pink ribbon or piece of pink twine around them. Over the course of five days, move them a little closer together every day, tightening the ribbon each time until they are eventually touching.

2. Leave them tied like this for seven days. By this time romance should have entered your life.

PURIFYING SPELL

Sometimes negative entities can attach
themselves to us, we can be aware or unaware of
this. They may show up and make your energy
feel stagnant, or you may feel extra tired. Their
heavy presence can make us late all the time,
cause creative blocks, or even be naughty and hide
things such as our keys. You have landed on this
page because it is more that likely you may have
been feeling some of these things. Purify your
home and notice the difference.

YOU WILL NEED:

four slices of lemon, salt, a plate

1. If you have any idea where the negative energy may have come from say it aloud over the lemons. If you don't, just skip to the next step, it's not a problem.

2. Cover the lemon slices entirely with salt.

3. Hold your hands over the plate and say:

'Uncrossed, uncrossed,
by the powers that be.
May this citrus soak up all negative
energy,unwelcome entities and spirits
leave me be.
As this lemon dries in salt and air,
I am freed from harm and despair.
Uncrossed and happy for all to see,
Blessed be and so mote it be.'

4. Leave this in a safe place for seven days (on top of a cupboard or on a bookshelf, out of the way). If in seven days everything has dried and the lemons are hard, the spell has worked.

5. If it is mouldy, you should repeat the spell again.

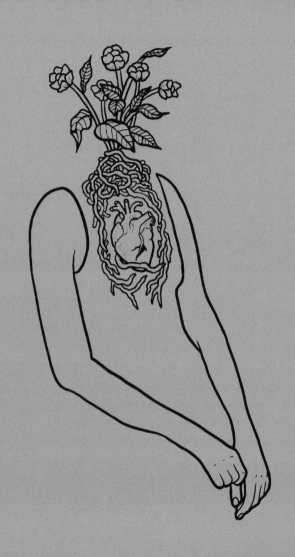

MAKE A WISH

Your wish is ready to be granted.

YOU WILL NEED
a large fresh leaf (don't forget to ask
for permission from the plant or tree before you
take the leaf), a black marker pen

1. Write out your wish on the leaf using
    the black marker pen.

2. Place the leaf in a safe place. When
    the leaf starts to dry, take it back to
    a large tree, crumple it up and offer it
    back to the earth at the base of
    the tree.

NEGATIVE ENERGY MUST BE REMOVED

There is a problem and it is holding you back
and taking up too much of your energy.

YOU WILL NEED

an old shoe, a black marker pen

1. On the bottom of your shoe, write out your problem using the black marker pen.

2. Put the shoe on and stamp it out.

3. Jump on it, slam it down – feel free to take some aggression out on it if needed!

4. Then take the shoe off and go and dispose of it in a bin far from your house.

A CALL FOR COURAGE

Your lack of courage is what is stopping you from achieving your goals. This can slow down or stop your intentions from coming to fruition. If your manifestations feel a little delayed, ask yourself if you are brave enough to step into the power of what you are calling in. Cloves are amazing little helpers – they bring bravery and the assurance that is needed right now.

YOU WILL NEED

a handful of cloves, a bowl, a red cloth or envelope to wrap the cloves in

1. Place a handful of cloves in a bowl on a windowsill, ideally facing east or in a spot that gets some sun.

2. Repeat this incantation three times over the cloves:

'Cloves of courage, make me brave,
may these magical cloves pave the way.
Faith and trust will come today,
may this magical feeling be here to stay.'

3. When the sun goes down, wrap them in the red cloth or red envelope.

4. Carry them around in your pocket or bag for a week.

INTUITION CHALLENGE: A BIRD

What does a bird mean to you?

How do you connect with this image?

If you are really stuck, turn to page 509 for some psychic prompts.

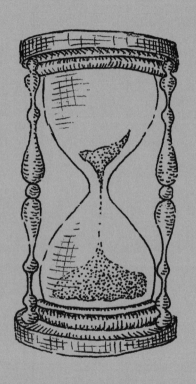

ASK AGAIN
TOMORROW.

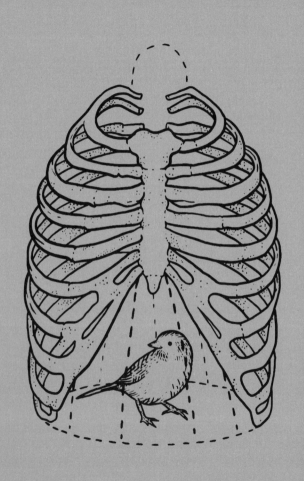

You are a gifted healer.
You have the power
shift the energy in a
room. You know how to
make people feel safe
and feel good about
themselves.

Embrace this magical
part of yourself and
share this energy –
the world needs more
people like you.

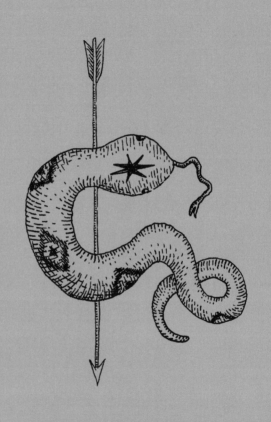

The Oracle needs a rest,
ask again in 10 minutes.

GIVE IT TIME.

222

You have been sent here
as you are being called
to check in with balance
in your life.

This could be with
friends, partners
or at work.

If the energy has felt
heavy, this can also be
a sign that things are
about to lighten up.

223

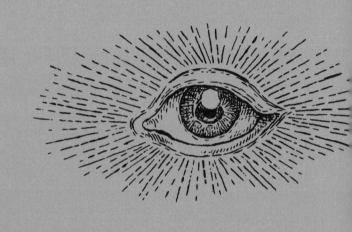

THE ORACLE
SAYS NO.

An old friend wants
to hear from you.
Call them up and share
a happy memory
with them.

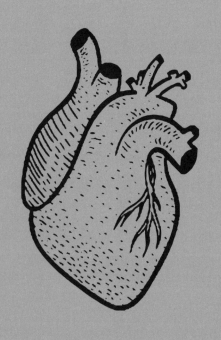

THE ORACLE IS ASKING YOU TO CONNECT WITH THE COLOUR PINK

The magical correspondence of the colour pink is calling you to connect with the magical power of love. This could be romantic love, love for your friendships or self- love.

The Oracle is advising you to practice optimism and self-care.

To connect to pink energy, you may choose to wear pink clothing, pink nails or pink lipstick. Wear this colour and remember all the times in life that things have worked out in your favour.

Think of all the people you love in your life and what you love about yourself.

1. Set a timer for 10 minutes. Close your eyes and visualise yourself with a pink fluffy aura surrounding you.

2. Summon a nurturing voice who speaks nothing but loving words of encouragement for the whole 10 minutes.

SLOW DOWN.

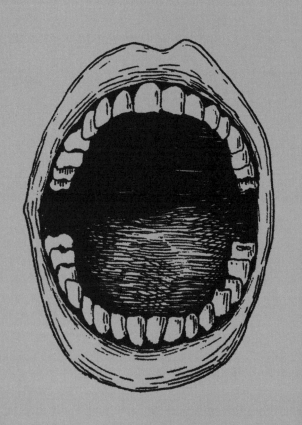

It's time to air
your opinions...

INTUITION CHALLENGE: SCALES

What does a set of scales mean to you?

How do you connect with this image?

If you are really stuck,
turn to page 509 for some psychic prompts.

THE ORACLE IS ASKING YOU TO CONNECT WITH THE COLOUR YELLOW

In magic, yellow brings abundance and happiness. Work with this colour to inspire your creative flow, clear any blocks that have been in your way and open the road to magical new opportunities.

1. To connect to this colour, you can wear an item of yellow clothing, tie some yellow string around your wrist, light a yellow candle or buy some yellow flowers.

2. As you work with this colour, tune in to the uplifting energy of the sun, feel its warmth and know that you are in harmony with the magic of the colour yellow.

REPEAT THE MANTRA:
'Colour of yellow,
inspire me with happiness,
joy and creativity.
Colour of sunshine, I feel thee,
bringing magic for all to see.'

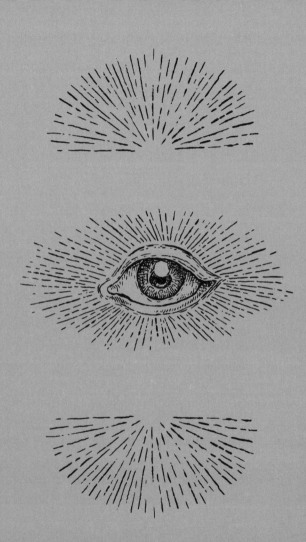

Invest in your future.

Every time you take a shower, visualise that you are washing away all of your stresses, sadness, despair and regret. Feel it all being washed away.

Let it all go down the drain.

Step out of the shower feeling lighter and cleansed.

ASK AGAIN.

YES,
YES,
YES.

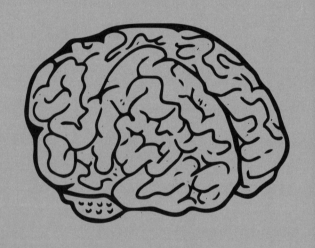

Remember:
the voice inside
your head
IS YOU.

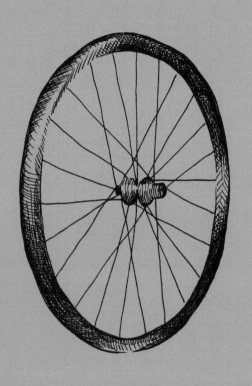

INTUITION
CHALLENGE:
A WHEEL

What does a wheel
mean to you?

How do you connect
with this image?

If you are really stuck, turn to page 509 for some
psychic prompts.

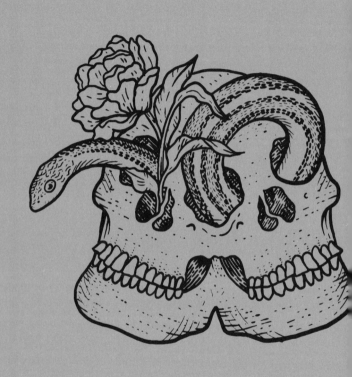

DEATH
=
REBIRTH

REBIRTH
=
DEATH

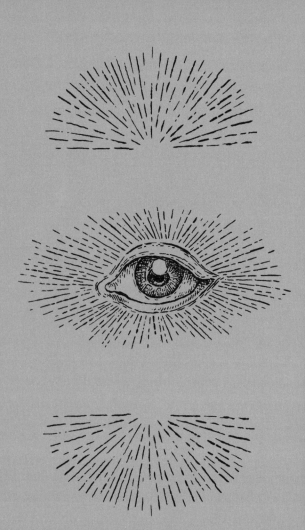

WHO AM I?

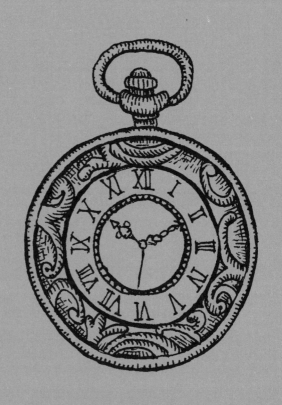

INTUITION
CHALLENGE:
A CLOCK

What does a clock
mean to you?

How do you connect
with this image?

If you are really stuck turn to page 509 for some
psychic prompts.

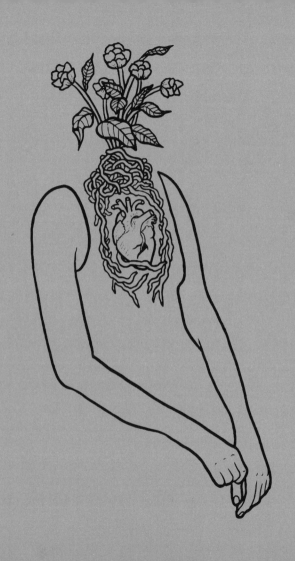

I AM _____

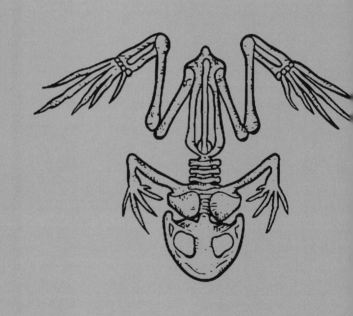

Boundaries must be
put into place and
respected.

RAISE YOUR
STANDARDS.

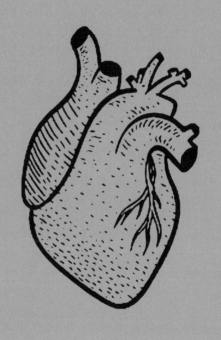

Expect everything
you have asked for to
start showing up in
unexpected ways.

Love yourself as
much as you desire
to be loved.

Logical doesn't
necessarily
mean beneficial.

Old narratives
don't belong in your
new life.

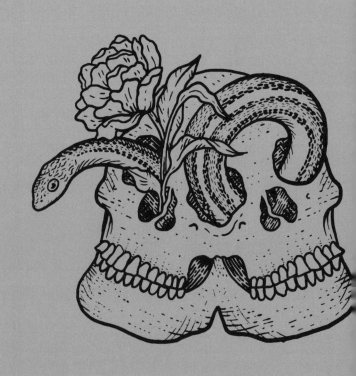

Is what is going
on inside as bright as
what you are showing
on the outside?

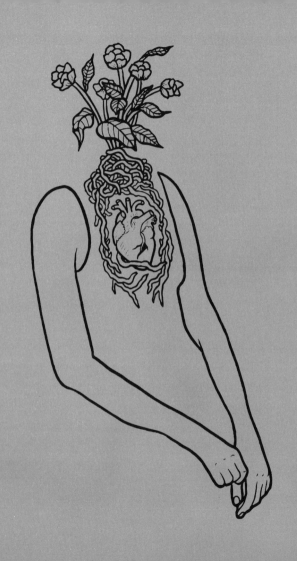

The same lessons will keep showing up until you have been taught what you need to know.

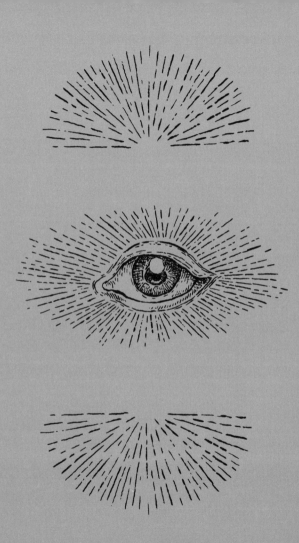

Mix things up –
wear something you
wouldn't usually
wear; eat something
you wouldn't usually
eat; watch a film you
wouldn't usually watch;
change your
morning routine.

You get the picture!

Create simple
shifts to shake up
stagnant energy.

MANIFEST
EXPANSION.

THE ORACLE IS ASKING YOU TO CONNECT WITH THE COLOUR BLUE

The magical correspondence of the colour blue is to bring calm and healing. You are being guided towards deep healing and inner peace.

If life has been hectic lately, tune in to the relaxing vibrations of the colour blue to help chill you out.

The Oracle wants to let you know that forgiveness sets your heart free.

Remember that forgiveness can be personal – you don't have to make contact with who may have upset you.

Close your eyes and imagine a blue light surrounding you.

REPEAT THE MANTRA:
'I have control over how I feel, and I choose to feel at peace.'

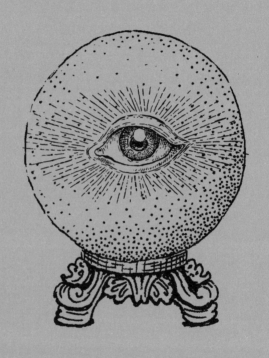

THIS PAGE IS
A GREEN LIGHT
(A BIG, BRIGHT,
NEON SPARKLY
ONE).

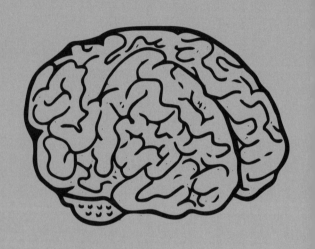

Having a different
perspective will help
right now.

OWN YOUR
POWER.

Everything is going to
be alright, the Universe
is making way for you
right now.

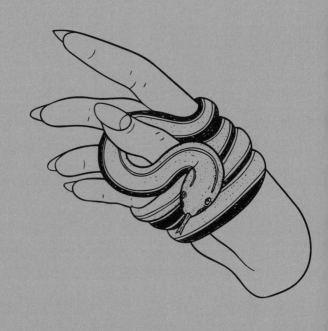

How are you expanding
your mind right now?

All of your hard work
will soon pay off.

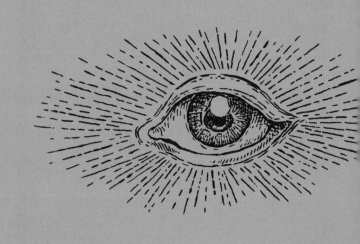

Keep your eyes
on the prizes.

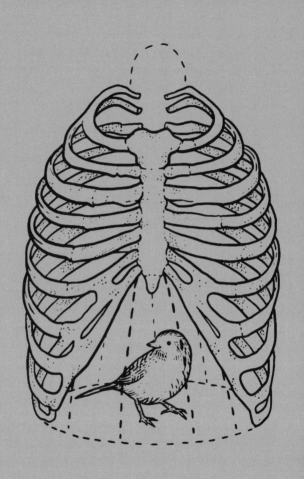

This is only
the beginning.

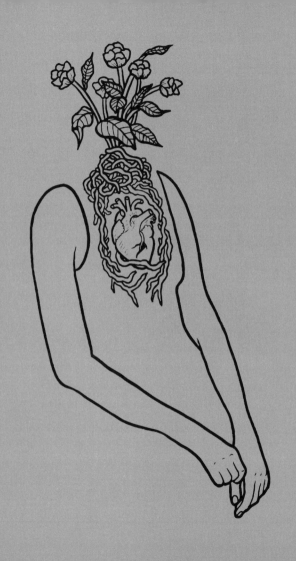

SHARE COSMIC ENERGY

Leave a cute note for a stranger, put it in an envelope and label it 'Dear Stranger'.

You can leave this note anywhere – on a car windscreen, on a seat on the bus, in a locker at the gym or hang it on a tree. If you are stuck for idea, you could try:

'Dear Stranger,
I just wanted to remind you that
you are significant, you are sparkly
and you add value to the world.'

'Dear Stranger,
Always remember:
You are a cosmic force.'

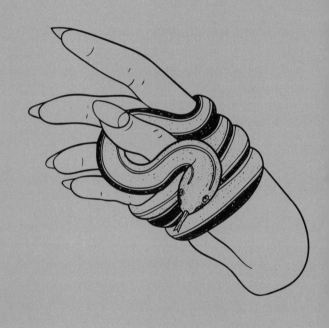

Your gut feeling
is correct.

Close your eyes and
see your future self
celebrating your
intentions coming
to fruition.

Work back and see
how you got there.
Now you know what
you've gotta do.

Imagine that you
are already there.
Close your eyes and
see it, smell it,
taste it, feel it.
It is yours.

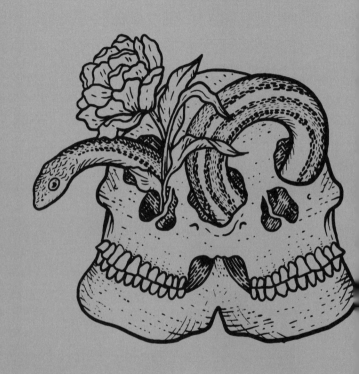

SURRENDER.

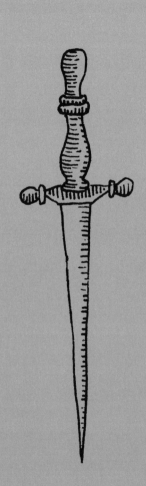

Stop putting that
thing off.

Stop fearing
your potential.

Pour love into
yourself and in turn,
the Universe will
pour love into you.

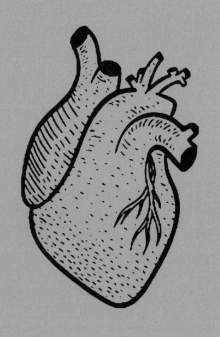

Your heart is mending
and deep healing is
taking place. Respect
that and be patient
with yourself.

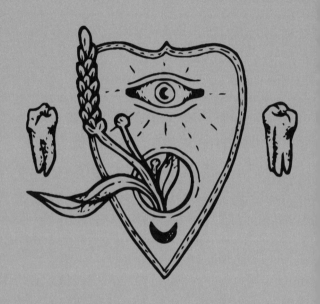

The love that you send
out into the world is
being noticed, it will
be coming back tenfold
very soon.

It is time to stop looking backward and start focusing on all that is to come. Recognise that what you went through has taught you many lessons.

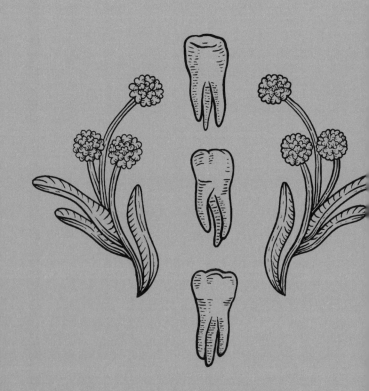

Remember, there is no light without dark.

Stop saying yes out
of obligation.

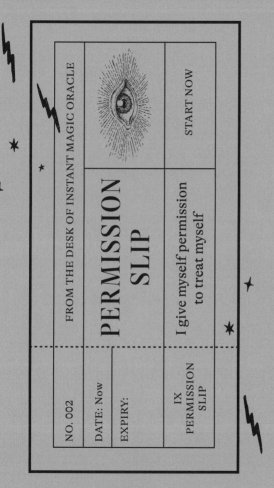

FROM THE DESK OF INSTANT MAGIC ORACLE

NO. 002

DATE: Now

EXPIRY:

PERMISSION SLIP

IX
PERMISSION
SLIP

I give myself permission
to treat myself

START NOW

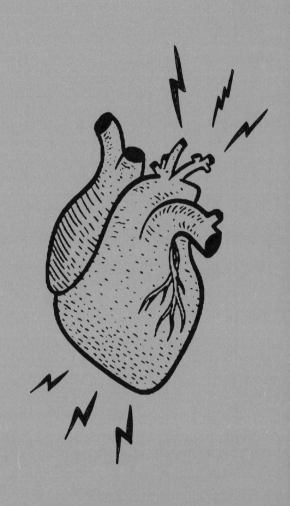

You win more hearts
than you know.

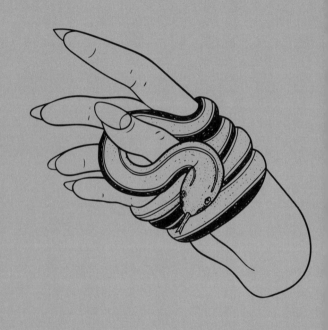

You don't have to be in
control of everything.

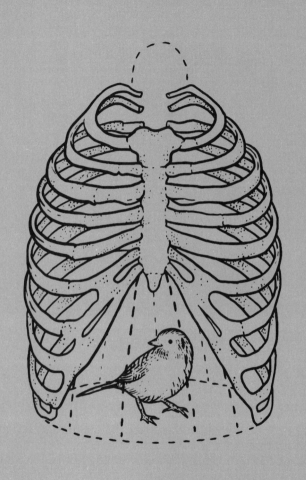

BEWARE OF TEMPTATION.

Beware of
outside opinions.
On this occasion,
keep your ideas and
plans to yourself.
Validation for these
ideas lies within.

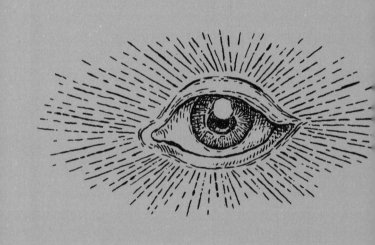

333

is here to tell you not
to give up. Keep going.
Major life changes
are ahead.

If you have been
working towards a goal,
completion and success
are on the way.

ASK A FRIEND.

Soon you will
be celebrating
a big win.

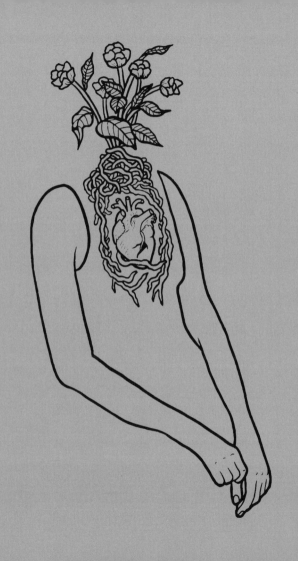

You are experiencing
spiritual growth
right now.

You may find that you
no longer have space
for certain friendships,
beliefs or old negative
thinking patterns.

Allow yourself to move
on; know that you are
creating space for
amazing new people,
new ways and
new energies.

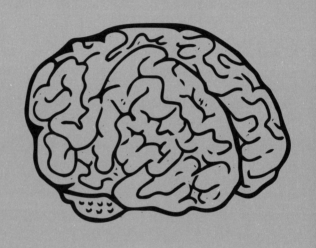

Switch the arguments you are playing over in your head to conversations that are filled with love, compassion and support.

INTUITION CHALLENGE: A BIRD

What does a bird mean to you?

How do you connect with this image?

If you are really stuck turn to page 509 for some psychic prompts.

ORACLE SAYS:
SNIP, SNIP, SNIP

There may be situations or people that you
wish you remove yourself from.

YOU WILL NEED

a white piece of paper, a pen, half a lemon,
scissors, matches or a lighter (optional)

1. On a white piece of paper, write your
   name in big letters and around it write
   out what you wish to remove. This
   could be an ex, hexes, debt, negative
   energy – whatever you can think of.

2. Then squeeze some lemon juice on
   the blades of some scissors and cut all
   the words away from your name. As
   you cut, feel a sense of relief of these
   things moving away from you.

3. Now cut those words into tiny pieces.

4. You can burn, flush or just chuck these
   in a bin.

5. Place the piece of paper with your
   name written on it on your altar or
   somewhere safe.

Don't worry about getting everything done this second. Relax, you'll be more productive in the long run.

Do not settle for
second best.

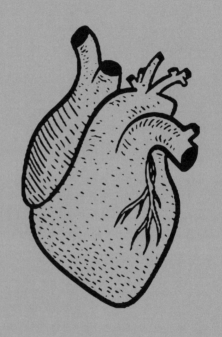

SPREAD LOVE

Spreading love and making people feel good creates magical energy that is filled with good vibes. When we share love and kindness it creates a ripple effect that spreads good vibes around the world.

Your challenge is to think of someone who you have gratitude for and write them a note telling them how grateful you are that they are in your life.

You can choose to email, text or even better, do it the old-fashioned way and post them a card or letter.

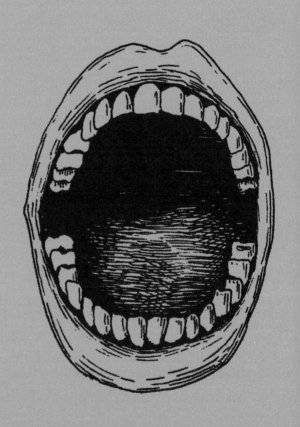

Celebrate your
last 10 wins ...
be sure to say them
out loud so the
Universe hears you.

Get that thing DONE.
Did you know that
avoiding doing
something takes up just
as much mental energy
as doing it? Here is your
prompt to get it done
and make some room
for MAGIC.

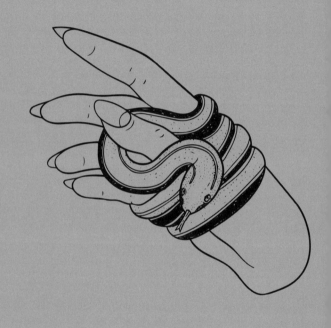

PLEASE KNOW THAT THERE ARE NO LIMITS

To fully realise this, do the following:

1. Sit in a quiet place and close your eyes.

2. Take in a big deep breath in.

3. Exhale a big breath out.

4. In your mind's eye, visualise a ceiling above your head.

5. Imagine a sledge hammer in your hand.

6. Look at the ceiling and know that it is representing the limitations you are putting on yourself.

7. Take the sledge hammer and visualise yourself smashing the ceiling up.

8. As you see yourself doing this, feel the limitations lifting; feel the blocks being removed and invite the inspiration and courage in.

9. See the sky through the broken ceiling.

10. Know that THE SKY IS THE LIMIT.

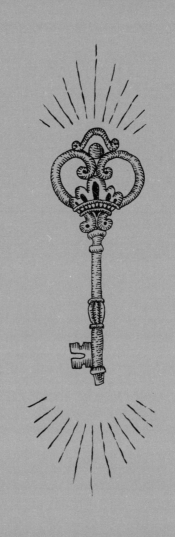

INTUITION CHALLENGE: A KEY

What does a key mean to you?

How do you connect with this image?

If you are really stuck, turn to page 509 for some psychic prompts.

Wear a ring on your ring finger to activate and inspire your creativity.

Acknowledge your
offerings to the world;
notice how they impact
your friends, family
and beyond. Know
that your energy has
an impact not only on
the community around
you, but on the rest of
the world. This is called
the ripple effect, and
you have the power to
spread positive, magical
vibes wherever you go.

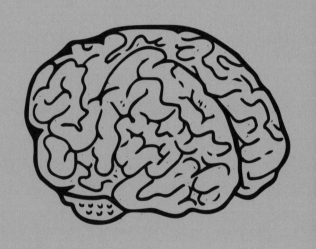

You may have a vision
of how you want things
to turn out, but you
have landed on this page
as a prompt to think
BIGGER!

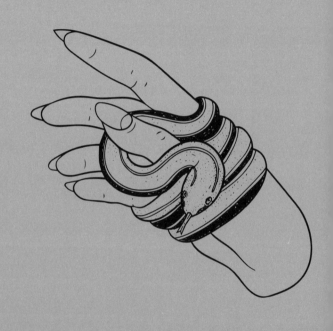

Solitude is needed.
Take a moment with
no energy other than
your own – turn off your
phone and take a break
from social media.
Be still and go within.

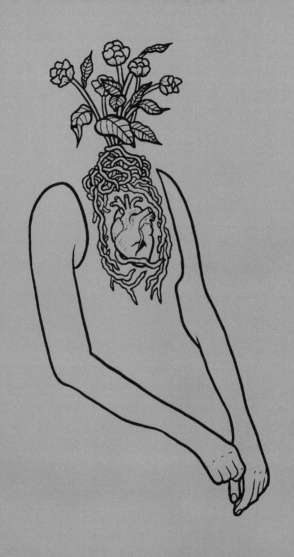

BY THE POWER OF THREE YOUR WISH SHALL COME TRUE

YOU WILL NEED

three bay leaves, a pen or pencil, parchment paper, matches or a lighter, a metal dish

1. Write out the same wish on three bay leaves.

2. Wrap them in parchment paper.

3. Burn them in the metal dish.

4. Scatter the ashes at your front door, ready to welcome your wishes home.

Stop conforming and start banging to the beat of your own drum. The time has come to do things in your own unique way.

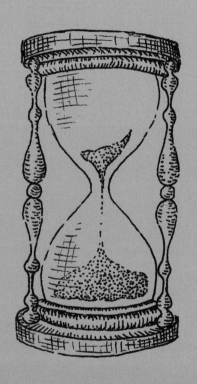

Close your eyes and see
the 18-year-old version
of yourself sitting in
front of you.

Tell them what they
need to know.

RETURN TO SENDER

It is time to send bad vibrations back to their
source. These may be from someone you know
– an enemy or a frenemy – or it might have been
some negative vibes that were floating around
that attached themselves to you.

YOU WILL NEED

a candle, matches or a lighter, a mirror,
dried sage or rosemary

1. Place the candle on a windowsill with
   the mirror behind it, facing outwards.

2. Light the candle and repeat three times:

   'Negative energy sent my way,
   the mirror reflects the sender's way.'

Let the candle burn until the end, then follow
up by burning some cleansing herbs such as sage
or rosemary.

INNER PEACE INCOMING

You may have had a disagreement or maybe
someone has upset or hurt you. If you want to
make peace but don't want to speak to them, you
can do it this way for guaranteed inner peace.

1. Sit in a quiet place and close your
   eyes. Picture somewhere in nature –
   this could be on a mountaintop, on a
   beach, in a forest or wherever else you
   may choose.

2. Once you have a clear picture in
   your head, visualise your higher-
   self walking from one side, and the
   other person's higher-self walking
   towards them. See your higher-selves
   meeting in the middle and imagine
   them talking to each other. Have a full
   conversation covering all areas you
   want to resolve.

3. Open your eyes. You should now feel
   some inner peace about the situation
   that was troubling you.

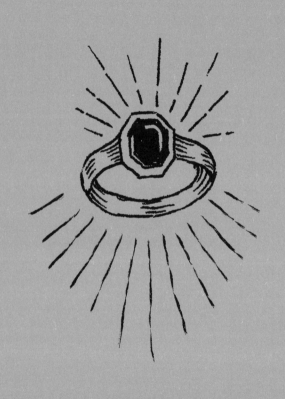

Wear a ring on your
little finger to improve
your communication.

IT IS TIME FOR
A PHONE CLEANSE

You may have had a negative phone call;
something on social media may have triggered
you; or maybe you received a call or message
that has upset you? Or perhaps you have a phone
addiction and can't stop scrolling?

Our phones can send out toxic vibes that can
permeate negativity in our energy field.

1.   Turn your phone off and hold your
     phone in your hands and repeat
     three times:

     'Negative energy from this device,
     I banish thee with pure white light.
     Phone calls and messages sent in spite,
     restore and reboot, I invite.
     Surround this phone in beams of protection,
     so that I have a will have
     a good connection.'

2.   Then close your eyes and visualise
     a cleansing and purifying white
     light beaming out of your hands and
     surrounding your phone.

3.   You can turn your phone back
     on, knowing that it has been
     spiritually reset.

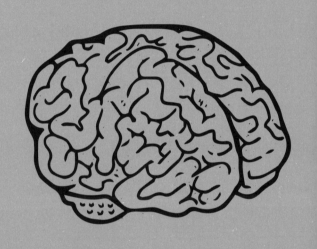

WELCOMING THE COSMIC CONTROL PANEL IN YOUR BRAIN...

1. Close your eyes and visualise a cockpit in a spaceship. Notice all of the switches, dials, buttons and levers.

2. Look a little closer and notice that above all of the controls are labels. You may notice a dial labelled with the word 'anxiety' and another switch labelled 'fear'. Maybe you see a dial which is labelled with 'self-worth' and another labelled with 'happiness'.

3. Now take a moment and notice how all of the switches are dialled, from 1, meaning low, to 10, meaning high.

4. When you have a clear vision, start adjusting them. Turn anxiety down to 2 and self-worth up to 10. Give all of the switches their own emotions and play around.

5. When you feel ready, open your eyes. Know that you can close your eyes and tune in to this cosmic control panel anytime you like.

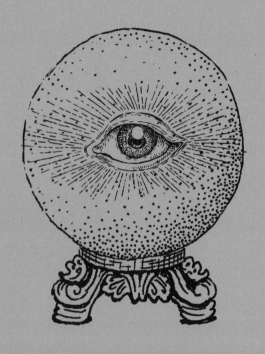

See the beauty in
EVERYTHING today.
Every. Single. Thing.

LIGHT A CANDLE, MAKE A WISH, GAZE INTO THE FLAME AND SAY:

'Magic flame that burns so bright,
bless my wishes that I write.
Magic candle I delight in thee,
please honour me. So mote it be.'

EXPECT
MIRACLES.

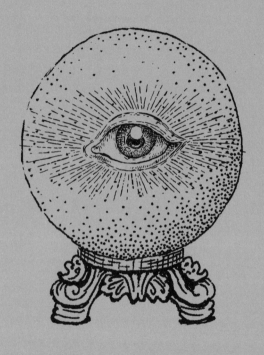

Someone is looking at
you and wishing they
had what you have.

YOU HAVE HEARD OF DANCING IT OUT, BUT NOW IT IS TIME TO DANCE IT IN

You are being called to choose your manifesting song.

1. Pick a song that lifts you up and makes you want to move your body.

2. Now pick one of your main manifestations of the moment.

3. Play the song and visualise what you are manifesting coming true.

4. Play the song loud and close your eyes and play the entire intention in your mind to the song.

5. As you dance, feel the energy around you, feel your vibration raising.

6. This is now your manifesting song. Every time you play it, dance and envision what you are calling in.

Sleep with a bunch of marjoram beneath your pillow to dream of love that is coming your way.

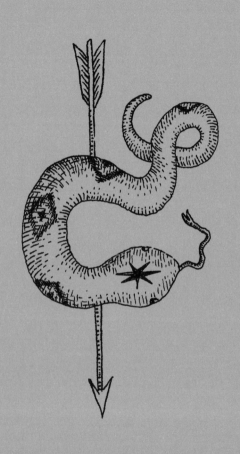

Peel a pear in one go, so that the entire peel is one long strip. Drop it on the floor and it will reveal the initial of the next person you will fall in love with.

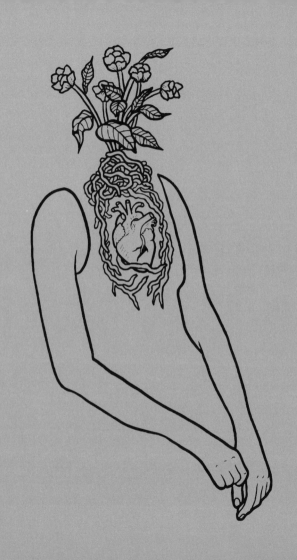

When we recognise our luck our vibrational frequency RAISES. Write down three times that you have experienced luck in your life.

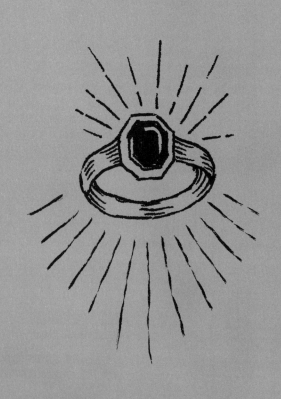

Wear a ring on your index finger to boost self-esteem.

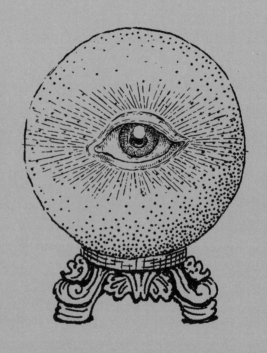

YOU ARE SEEKING AN ANSWER THAT ONLY A MAGIC SPELL CAN ANSWER

YOU WILL NEED

a blank sheet of paper, a pen, a candle, matches or a lighter

1. Write out your question on a piece of paper, then carve the first letter from each word of your question onto a candle.

2. Light the candle, burn the paper and by the time the candle has burned all the way down you will have your answer. (You can relight the candle over seven days if you need to.)

There may be someone or a situation that you wish to freeze out of your life. Write the problem or the person's name on a piece of paper and simply put it in the ice container in the freezer. Keep them in there and freeze them out for as long as you need to.

PROTECTION IS NEEDED

YOU WILL NEED
a glass jar, a handful of nails, some water

1. Fill a glass jar with a handful of nails and then top it up with water.

2. Leave it in a dark place for a week until the nails start to rust.

3. Once the water is a little rusty, either sprinkle a few drops outside your home for protection or pour over your fingers before any confrontations.

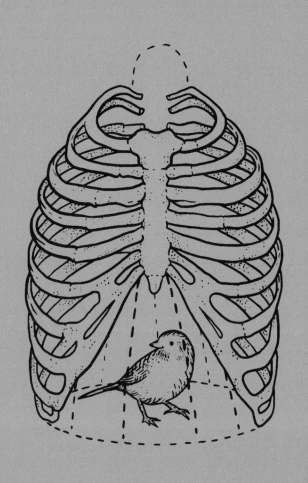

MAKE A SMALL PROMISE TO YOURSELF RIGHT NOW AND INTRODUCE A DAILY RITUAL INTO YOUR LIFE

1. It could be as small as drinking a glass of water as soon as you wake up everyday or promising to free write every morning.

2. Promise that you will do it every day for the next 30 days.

3. Put a reminder in your calendar so you can check back in 30 days.

Know that you are not
the only one who feels
like an impostor.

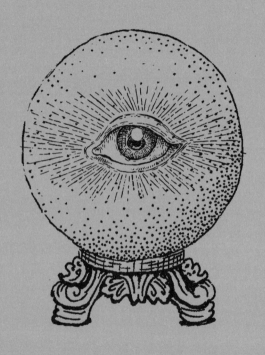

Trust in the divine
timing of everything.
Delays, obstacles, hold-
ups and detours might
be happening for
a reason.

All you have to do
is show up.

For a different outcome,
challenge yourself with
the way you respond.

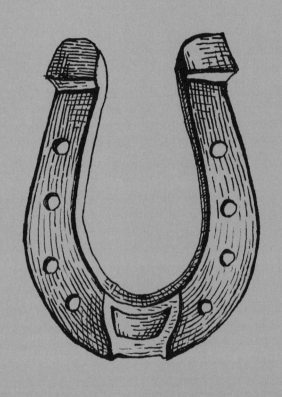

LUCK INCOMING

The Oracle says you are due some luck.
It is recommended that you boost your
incoming blessings.

YOU WILL NEED

a large bowl or vessel, chamomile tea

1. Brew a vessel of chamomile tea.
    As you steep the chamomile, stir in
    a clockwise direction, programming
    it with what you wish it to bring you
    luck with.

2. When the tea has cooled down, bathe
    your hands in it and visualise what
    luck you would like this chamomile to
    bring your way.

(Chamomile is very lucky. You can also wash the
entrance to your house with this mixture to bless
your home with luck.)

If you feel that someone is messing with your energy, relax in the comfort that they have no idea who is protecting you.

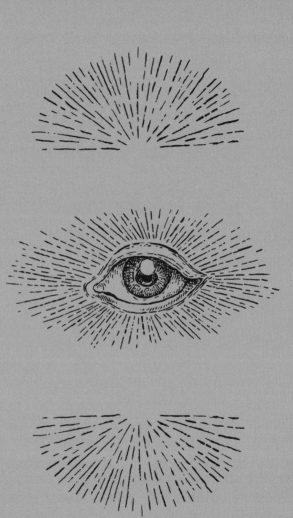

You keep
repeating harmful
behaviours.

Ask yourself why.

YOU ARE
A MIRROR.

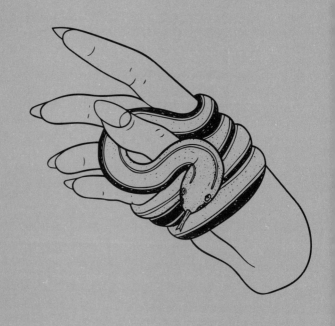

JUST BE
YOURSELF.

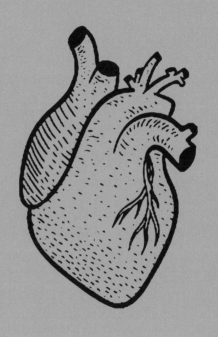

With darkness
comes light.

Connect to your shadow
self: light a candle for it,
understand it and show
it compassion.

Remember:
the Universe will
never present you with
something that you
can't handle.

IT IS TIME TO LET GO

The blame and anger that you are carrying
around is preventing you from moving forward.

YOU WILL NEED

a piece of white paper, a pen, a black candle,
some matches or a lighter, some salt

1. Write your worries on a piece of paper
    and fold the paper as small as possible,
    noticing your worries minimising as
    you fold.

2. Next, light a black candle facing
    north and burn the paper over the
    candle flame.

3. Blend the ashes with the salt to
    purify them.

YOUR NEXT
MOVE IS VITAL.

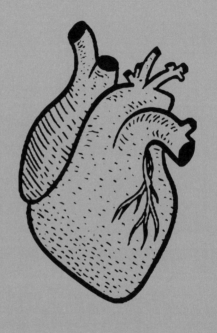

LISTEN TO
YOUR HEART.

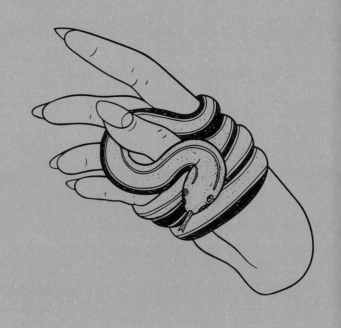

The element of air blows out the old and in the new. Think about what you wish to release and what you wish to call in.

Write a list of the things that no longer bring you happiness.

Face east and burn them, then write down all the joys you wish the magical winds to blow in your direction.

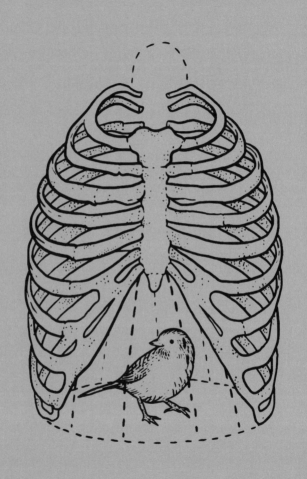

Just be true to yourself
and everything
will work out.

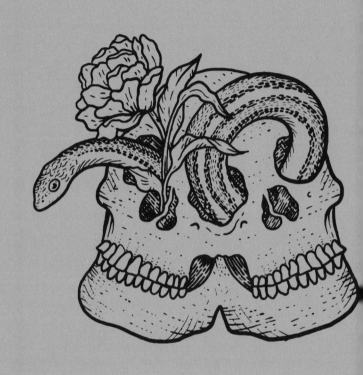

Go easy on yourself,
things needn't be
so difficult.

Stop with the
comparison to others,
you are on your own
path and they are
on theirs.

444

The Oracle says:
GREEN LIGHT GO-GO-GO!

These page numbers show you that
you have nothing to fear.

The numbers 444 are here to tell
you to have confidence in where
you are at and what you are doing.

They signify any action that is
taken now will be hugely successful
for you.

Music is the answer. Put on your
favourite song and dance.

No need to rush, sometimes it's
better to walk than to run.

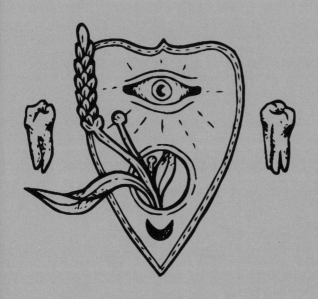

445

Patterns repeat
until lessons have
been learnt.

CLEAR THINKING IS NEEDED

You need to pay closer attention.

YOU WILL NEED

a piece of paper, a pen, some dried mint leaves

1. Put a pen and some paper in your pocket. Sprinkle some dried mint leaves in your shoes and go for a walk with your phone switched off.

2. As you walk, ask to be led in the right direction or think of any questions you may have.

3. Take in your surroundings – notice the smells, what you see, what you hear, and look out for any signs.

4. Feel free to stop and make note of anything that might be relevant.

5. By the time you come home you will have a clearer vision than before you left.

Retreat, solitude is
calling you. Avoid loud
places and be still in
peace. Sit back
and rejuvenate.

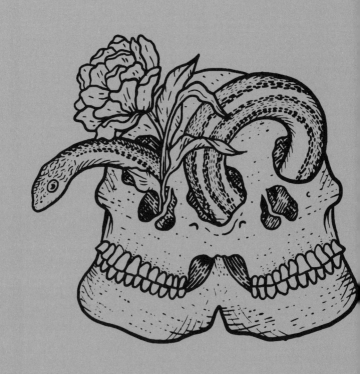

You are only making
excuses to yourself.

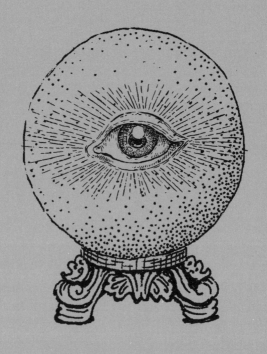

DOUBLE-CHECK
FACTS.

DISRUPTING PATTERNS

+

REPROGRAMMING
PREDICTABILITY

=

A DIFFERENT OUTCOME.

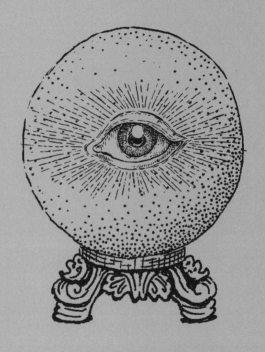

YOU HAVE THE POWER
TO MAKE MAGIC
HAPPEN.

REMEMBER THE
FORMULA:

INTENTION + ACTION
=
MAGIC

Place a pinch of thyme
and a pinch of marjoram
into a pot of honey to
inspire your creativity.
Bless it beneath the
new moon's energy.
Wake up in the morning
and eat a spoonful, then
write in your journal.
Do this for seven days
and your creative juices
will be flowing.

STRIKE A MATCH
AND OBSERVE
THE SMOKE:

1. If it travels up, the energy is clear.

2. If it travels north, trust your wisdom.

3. If it travels south, healing is needed.

4. If it travels east, energy is
   passing through.

5. If it travels west, tune in to
   your emotions.

THE COURAGE TO TAKE
A RISK IS IN YOUR
FAVOUR RIGHT NOW

YOU WILL NEED

a white candle, some olive or almond oil,
dried thyme, matches or a lighter

1. Anoint a white candle with some oil
   (olive or almond would be best).

2. Roll your candle in dried thyme.

3. Light the candle and gaze at the
   flame. As you gaze in to the flame,
   think of someone you know who
   has taken a risk and had it pay off.
   This could be someone you know
   or someone you admire; it could be
   someone you know personally, a
   friend of a friend or someone famous.

4. As you gaze in to the flame,
   see this person's face and tune in
   to their energy.

5. When you feel connected to this
   energy, ask for it to bring you the
   courage you need to take the risk
   that is on your mind.

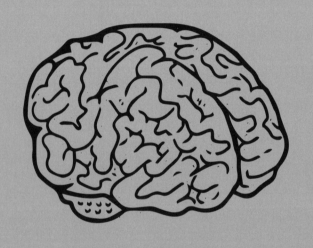

ESCAPE ROOM

1. Get comfy, close your eyes and visualise your home. Spend some time thinking of about the space and how you know it so well.

2. As you are seeing all of the familiarities, notice a door somewhere that you've not seen before.

3. Walk over to the door and open it.

4. Beyond the door is a space that you didn't know existed. Feel the surprise that this room has been there all along and you had no idea!

5. Walk around the room and inspect it. Be in awe of how beautiful the interiors are. Notice all of the details, colour schemes, furnishings; feel how incredible the energy is in this space. Spend some time here, soak it up.

6. Know that you can pop back to this room anytime you like.

LOST AND FOUND

You might have lost an item recently,
the Oracle wants to help you find it.

YOU WILL NEED

two small mirrors, two white tealight candles or
candles with holders, matches or a lighter

1. Stand the mirrors together so that
    they are both reflecting outwards.

2. Light the candles at either side of the
    mirrors. Visualise the mirrors sending
    out a light and it guiding you to the
    lost item and then visualise the lost
    item gravitating toward the mirrors.

3. Do the same thing the following few
    days and repast the visualisation.

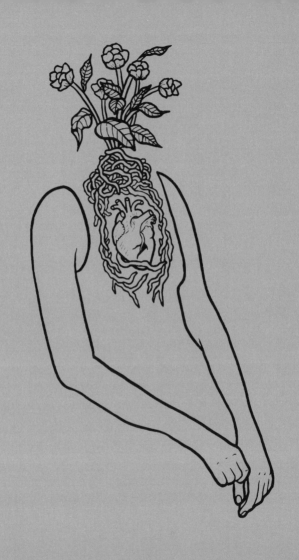

A GRATITUDE JAR

YOU WILL NEED
strips of paper, a pen, an empty jar

1. Write out on 10 strips of paper what you are grateful for and put them in an empty jar.

2. Add a few strips everyday.

3. When you have been doing this for 30 days, write a page of wishes.

4. Put the piece of paper with your wishes in the jar with all of the things you are grateful for. Place the jar out overnight to be charged under the full moon.

5. Wait for your wishes to come true!

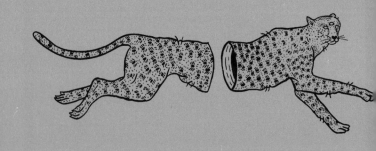

GROUNDING
IS NEEDED

You may have found yourself experiencing indecisiveness or a sense of confusion lately. We often feel like this when we are off balance.

When we are grounded, our bodies feel centred, which brings with it a higher level of self-assurance, and we see things with a clearer vision.

To restore balance and grounding:

1. Take a pinch of salt and a pinch of soil blend in a clockwise direction.

2. Sprinkle a little of the mixture on the top of each foot and stand tall with your arms beside you.

3. Rock back and forth and side to side for a few minutes, so the soles of your feet are touching the ground.

4. Feel the grounding energy of the spell pushing your feet down so that they are firmly on the ground.

REMEMBER:
EVERYTHING
IS ENERGY

1. Sit comfortably, with both feet firmly on the ground. Place your palms together and start rubbing your hands at a steady pace for about 20–30 seconds (or until they are nice and warm).

2. Slowly start to move your hands apart, and every time you move them apart move them a little closer together again. You should be feeling an energy pull starting to form between your hands.

3. As you continue to do this, feel yourself creating the shape of a ball. Spend some time focusing on moulding your energy ball.

4. Think of an intention, say it in to the ball and then throw the ball out in to the world.

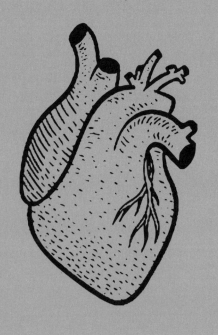

UNCONDITIONAL LOVE FOREVER

Allow your intuition to guide you to the most magical
unconditional love

1. Close your eyes and imagine what it would be like
   to receive the most nurturing and unconditional
   love you have ever felt.

2. Now visualise the being who is radiating this
   magical love to you. This could be a human, an
   animal, someone who has passed, half man/half
   cat, a gorilla or even an alien!!! Go with whatever
   the first being that you saw.

3. Now see them looking at you and smiling. See
   the love in their eyes – they adore you, they want
   nothing but the best for you. They see all of your
   potential and in their eyes you can do know wrong.

4. When you have a clear picture of them, ask them
   what their name is. And then allow them to
   shower you with compliments, of which they have
   an abundance of.

5. Soak up all of the lovely things they have to say to
   you. Have a cuddle with them if you like!

6. Know that you can call in on them whenever you
   need some love or encouragement. All you have to
   do it close your eyes and you will see them there.

THE ORACLE WANTS TO CONNECT WITH THE MAGICAL ELEMENT OF WATER.

WATER PURIFIES AND BRINGS PEACE

1. Face west and hold a cup of water.

2. Think about an area of your life that is calling for a little cleansing and healing.

3. Place your hands on the cup of water and say:

   'Water bring me peace I seek,
   cleanse, purify and heal,
   from my head to my feet.'

4. Drink the cup of water. Feel its magical cleansing energy refresh and purify you.

Place a yellow flower
under your pillow to
restore your energy.

To unlock the path ahead, charge a shiny key up in the sunlight and then anoint it with sunflower oil.

Sleep with it beneath your pillow to bring inspiration of how to unlock your dreams.

TALK LIKE
AN ANGEL:

When angels talk it is
so sweet. Kind, loving
and gentle.

Make a promise to talk
to yourself like this for
the next 24 hours.

THE ORACLE IS ASKING YOU TO CONNECT WITH THE COLOUR RED

In magic, red invokes passion and power.
Connect to the magical energy of the colour red
and call in your superpower and ignite
your passion.

Perhaps you have been feeling uninspired or
maybe your sexual desires have been a little flat.
Call in red to banish those lackluster vibes and
awaken some excitement and fervour. To do this,
wear something red – this could be clothing,
lipstick or lighting a red candle (if you light a red
candle, light it facing south in the direction of
fire for extra oomph).

As you light your candle or put on your red
clothing, repeat the mantra below.

REPEAT THIS MANTRA THREE TIMES:

'Power of red, bring to me,
power and passion for all to see.
Awaken my courage and let my willpower be,
I acknowledge all the excitement that
red brings to me.
Bless this magical colour with
the power of three,
I declare, so mote it be.'

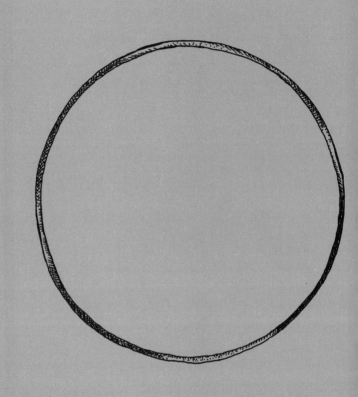

INTUITION
CHALLENGE:
A CIRCLE

What does a circle
mean to you?

How do you connect
with this image?

If you are really stuck, turn to page 509 for some psychic prompts.

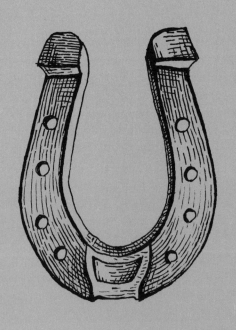

THE ORACLE IS ASKING YOU TO CONNECT WITH THE COLOUR ORANGE

In magic, orange is associated with vitality and courage; it brings luck and boosts your ambition. The Oracle may have directed you here because you may be in need of a little bit of orange to lift your mood and shift some stagnant energy to help you reach your goals.

Allow the magical properties of orange to give you a little injection of enthusiasm.

Embrace orange by wearing an item of orange clothing, or tying a piece of orange string around your wrist. Or eat an orange with a firm intention of how you would like the colour to work for you.

THE SPIRIT OF INQUIRY
IS CALLING YOU

What is it that you
would like to
learn more about?

What inspires
your curiosity?

Learning new things
will give you a new
found energy and
the passion you have
been craving.

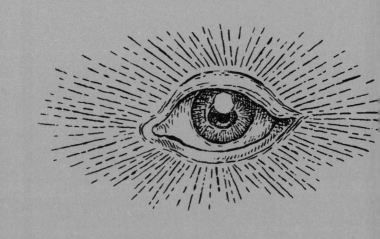

KEEP THE FAITH.

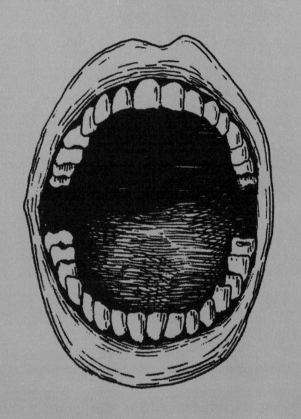

SPEAK YOUR MANIFESTATIONS INTO EXISTENCE

Arrange a date with a friend – this could be in person or on the phone – and talk like you are in the future.

1. Pick how far in the future you want to be (six months to one year is best).

2. Speak about all the things that you have going on in your life at this point in the future. Talk about how all of your manifestations and dreams came to fruition.

Note: this is tried and tested and super powerful, so take some time beforehand to go over the finer details. Make sure your friend is on-board too.

Wear a ring on your middle finger to help with anxiety.

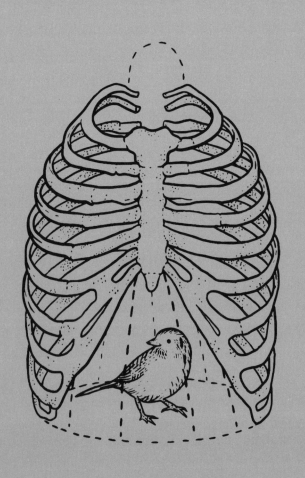

THE ORACLE IS ASKING YOU TO CONNECT WITH THE COLOUR WHITE

This will enable you to gain clarity and bring light to a challenge or obstacle that you have been waiting for clearance on.

The Oracle is guiding you to connect with white to purify your energy and invoke truth.

When you come out of the shower, wear some white clothes and burn some purifying herbs like sage or rosemary.

Challenge yourself to set a brand new intention (one that you have never made before).

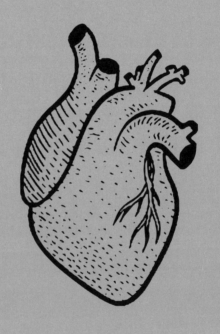

SWEET LOVE
MAGIC

To call in love,
burn some sugar
on a hot charcoal disc
while facing south.
As the smoke travels,
say:

'Sugar so sweet, burning
on this heat. Bring me a
love that will make my
heart skip a beat.'

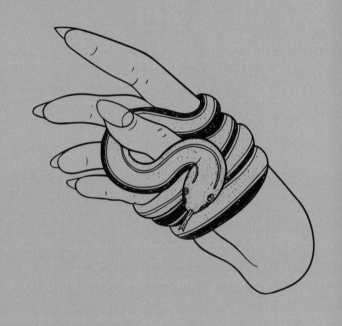

PASSIONATE
INTENTIONS INCOMING

Fire awakens desire and
inspiration. Create an
altar facing south, place
a candle (preferably
red) at the centre of
the altar. Manifest
courage and your most
passionate intentions
while calling in the
power of this element.

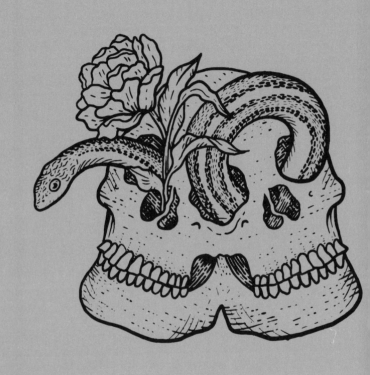

There is always another
side of the story,
remember that.

INTUITION
CHEAT SHEET

Welcome to the cheat sheet. You may have turned to this page because you were unable to tune into what the symbol could mean, or maybe you are looking for confirmation of your interpretation.

Before you read any further, try to think what your very first thought was when you saw the image. Remember that our intuition is our instinct and often our answer lies within our immediate first response.

RING

Devotion.

Commitment.

Love.

You will be asked to keep a promise.

Wholesomeness.

SUITCASE

Freedom.

What needs to be packed away or unpacked.

Hidden thoughts.

Moving.

Travel.

COFFIN

An ending and a beginning.

Time to break a negative habit.

Leaving the old behind.

Acceptance.

Challenging yourself to talk about difficult feelings.

DOOR

Transition from one place to another.

Endings and beginnings.

The known and the unknown.

Secrets and mystery.

To try harder.

Knocking on many doors.

A new way of doing things.

CIRCLE

Wholeness.

Completion.

Life lessons.

Challenging times.

BIRDS

Strength.

Fertility.

Protection.

Productivity.

An important message
is on the way.

WHEEL

Movement.

Repeating patterns/
breaking patterns.

Starting a project
(wheels in motion).

Time to start a project.

Rapid change is incoming.

CLOCK

Structure.

Speed up.

Slow down.

Look at your schedule.

A situation that cannot
be avoided.

SCALES

Transitions.

Be open to change.

Finding balance.

Feminine and masculine
energies should be looked at.

Work/life balance.

Look after your health.

KEY

New beginnings.

Boundaries.

Unlocking the subconscious.

Achievement of goals.

A spiritual awakening.

A new home.

ABOUT THE AUTHOR

Semra Haksever is an eclectic witch.

She has been fascinated and practising all things metaphysical for over 20 years.

Semra believes that a leap of faith into the unknown and a little magic can open the doors to possibilities, empower and create powerful transformations.

Inspired by this belief, in 2015 she created Mama Moon Candles, a bespoke collection of candles, potions and magical tools all made with the intention to make magic and rituals accessible to all.

Semra has a shop in East London, where she hosts moon rituals and spell-making workshops.

This is her fourth book.

@mamamooncandles
www.mamamooncandles.com

510

ACKNOWLEDGEMENTS

Thank you to Kate for giving me this amazing
opportunity and believing in my kind of magic!

This book is dedicated to the amazing,
supportive, courageous and inspirational
women in my life.

Special shout out to,
Mummy, Suwindi and Cairine –
I love you. xxx

Published by OH Editions
20 Mortimer Street
London W1T 3JW

Design © OH Editions

ISBN 978-1-914317-02-6

Text © Semra Haksever

Illustrations on pages 10—12, 20, 24, 30—34, 38—40, 44—60,
66—76, 82—90, 94, 98, 102—104, 108, 112—18, 122—24,
132—36, 142, 146—54, 158—60, 164, 168—74, 178—80,
186—88, 194, 198—202, 206—10, 216, 220, 223, 226—30,
236, 240—45, 250, 256—272, 276—78, 282—90, 294—98,
302—304, 308—18, 324—50, 354—56, 362—70, 376,
380—82, 386—88, 392—94, 398, 404—10, 414—16, 420,
426—452, 456, 462—66, 470—86, 492, 500—506
© Nes Vuckovic
All other llustrations © Evi O Studios
Design: Evi-O. Studio | Evi O., Nicole Ho,
Susan Le, Kait Polkinghorne, Wilson Leung

Production: Rachel Burgess

A CIP catalogue record for this book is available from
the British Library

Printed and bound in China

10 9 8 7 6 5 4